COOL CARS

PORSCHE

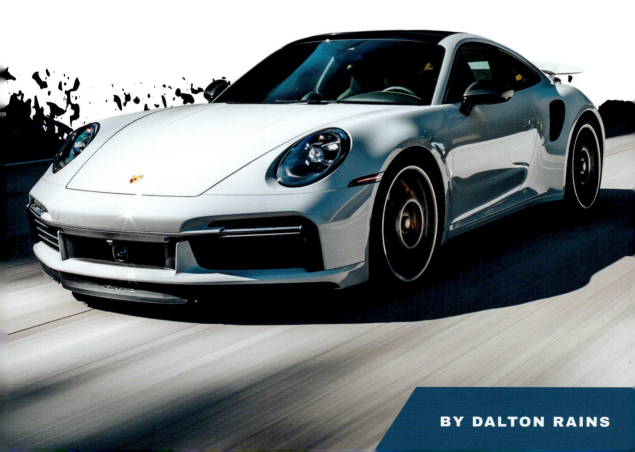

BY DALTON RAINS

WWW.APEXEDITIONS.COM

Copyright © 2026 by Apex Editions, Mendota Heights, MN 55120. All rights reserved. No part of this book may be reproduced or utilized in any form or by any means without written permission from the publisher.

Apex is distributed by North Star Editions:
sales@northstareditions.com | 888-417-0195

Produced for Apex by Red Line Editorial.

Photographs ©: Pixabay, cover; Shutterstock Images, 1, 4–5, 8, 12, 13, 16–17, 18–19, 20–21, 22–23, 25, 29; Loredana Sangiuliano/SOPA Images/Sipa USA/AP Images, 6–7; Malcolm Griffiths/LAT Images//Formula E/Getty Images, 9; National Motor Museum/Heritage Images/Hulton Archive/Getty Images, 10–11; iStockphoto, 14–15; Zhe Ji/Getty Images News/Getty Images, 24; JT/picture-alliance/dpa/AP Images, 26–27

Library of Congress Control Number: 2025930934

ISBN
979-8-89250-526-0 (hardcover)
979-8-89250-562-8 (paperback)
979-8-89250-633-5 (ebook pdf)
979-8-89250-598-7 (hosted ebook)

Printed in the United States of America
Mankato, MN
082025

NOTE TO PARENTS AND EDUCATORS

Apex books are designed to build literacy skills in striving readers. Exciting, high-interest content attracts and holds readers' attention. The text is carefully leveled to allow students to achieve success quickly. Additional features, such as bolded glossary words for difficult terms, help build comprehension.

TABLE OF CONTENTS

CHAPTER 1
Lightning Fast 4

CHAPTER 2
History 10

CHAPTER 3
Main Cars 16

CHAPTER 4
Other Cars 22

COMPREHENSION QUESTIONS • 28
GLOSSARY • 30
TO LEARN MORE • 31
ABOUT THE AUTHOR • 31
INDEX • 32

CHAPTER 1

LIGHTNING FAST

Pascal Wehrlein speeds down a racetrack. His all-electric Porsche is in fourth place. But he needs to move up. He's racing in the **Formula E** World **Championship**.

Pascal Wehrlein drove the Porsche 99X Electric during the 2024 Formula E championship.

The 99X Electric can reach 60 miles per hour (97 km/h) in about two seconds.

FAST FACT

The 2024 Formula E championship took place in London, England. Drivers raced through city streets.

Wehrlein swerves through narrow turns. Then he takes an inside corner. The Porsche moves to third place.

Wehrlein scored the most points across all the Formula E races in 2024.

Wehrlein slams down on the **accelerator**. The Porsche's motors whir. The car zooms to second place. That is enough to **clinch** the season. Wehrlein is a champion!

GREAT RACERS

Over the years, Porsche has won thousands of races. That includes many victories at Le Mans. In Le Mans, drivers race for 24 hours straight.

A few months after Porsche won the 2024 Formula E title, the company released the new 99X Electric Gen3.

CHAPTER 2

History

Ferdinand Porsche was an **engineer** and **mechanic**. In the 1930s, he and his son started a car company. Porsche came out with its first sports car in 1948. It was the Porsche 356.

Ferdinand Porsche made the first Porsche 356s in Austria. The cars were lightweight and fast.

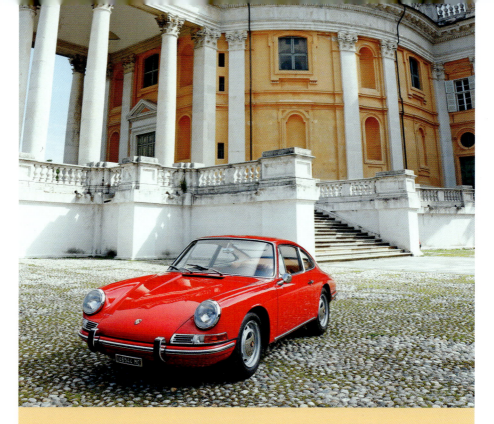

The original Porsche 911 had a top speed of 130 miles per hour (210 km/h).

In 1963, Porsche showed the 911 to the world. It became an instant success. Porsche updated the 911 line often over the years.

FAST FACT
The Porsche 930 sold from 1975 to 1989. It was one of the fastest **production cars** available.

The 930 was the first production car with a turbocharged engine. This engine gave it massive power.

The Panamera was a four-door sports car. It featured both space and speed.

SUVs

Porsche's first SUV came out in 2002. It was called the Cayenne. In 2013, the company added the smaller Macan. Both SUVs were roomy and comfortable.

The Panamera hit the roads in 2009. It was Porsche's first **sedan**. By then, Porsche had options for many kinds of drivers.

CHAPTER 3

MAIN CARS

The Porsche 911 remained popular into the 2020s. Its engine was at the back of the car. Heavy weight on the rear wheels helped with acceleration and braking.

The Porsche 911 was known for its dramatic sloping front, circle-shaped headlights, and powerful engine.

The Carrera was the starting 911 model. But drivers had plenty of choices. The Turbo featured lots of power. The Targa and Cabriolet sported open tops.

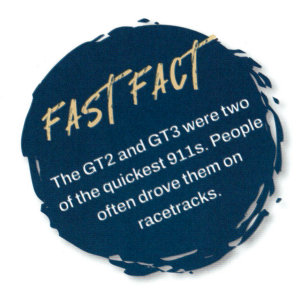

FAST FACT

The GT2 and GT3 were two of the quickest 911s. People often drove them on racetracks.

One type of 911 Turbo S could reach 205 miles per hour (330 km/h).

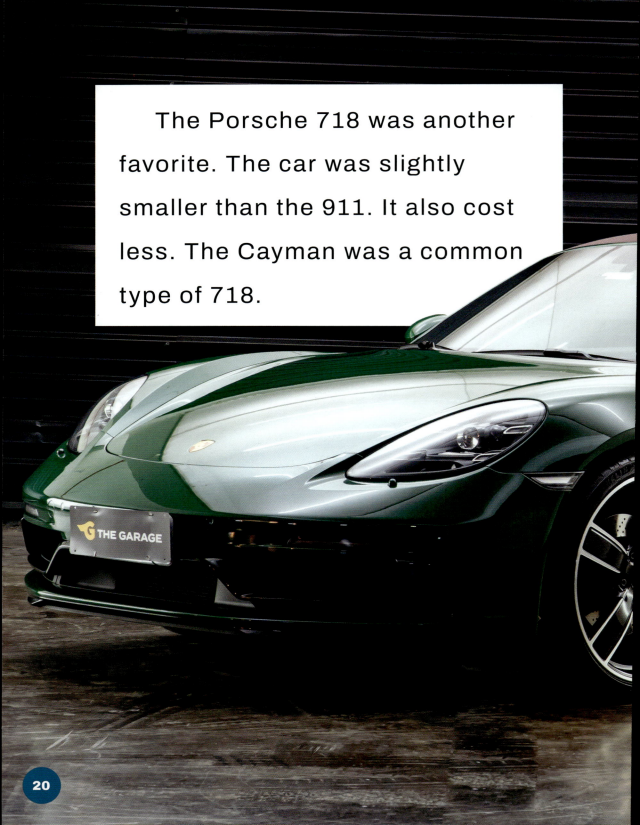

The Porsche 718 was another favorite. The car was slightly smaller than the 911. It also cost less. The Cayman was a common type of 718.

The 718 was a mid-engine car. The engine sat behind the seats but in front of the rear wheels.

STYLE AND SPEED

Porsche sold several varieties of 718. The GTS had the most power. The Style Edition showed off striking colors and bodywork. People could also get an open-top 718.

CHAPTER 4

Other Cars

Porsche made many other vehicles, too. Some sold widely. The Taycan was one popular car. It was all-electric.

A Taycan could charge its battery most of the way in just 18 minutes.

The Vision 357 celebrated 75 years since the launch of the Porsche 356.

Other Porsches were rare. The Vision 357 came out in 2023. This **concept car** had smooth curves. And it had flashy paintwork.

ELECTRIC RACER

The Porsche Mission R was another concept car. This race car was all-electric. It could go more than 186 miles per hour (300 km/h).

The Porsche Mission R featured racing display screens and a clear roof.

Porsche kept building successful race cars, too. The Porsche 963 began racing in the early 2020s. Fans couldn't wait for the next Porsches to hit the track and the road.

FAST FACT

The Porsche 963's shape and color were based on the 917. A 917 gave Porsche its first win at Le Mans.

The Porsche 963 won many races in 2024. It came in first at the 24 Hours of Daytona world championship.

COMPREHENSION QUESTIONS

Write your answers on a separate piece of paper.

1. Write a few sentences explaining the main ideas of Chapter 2.

2. Which Porsche model would you most like to have? Why?

3. What year did Porsche release its first SUV?
    - A. 2002
    - B. 2009
    - C. 2013

4. Which of these Porsches came out most recently?
    - A. Vision 357
    - B. Panamera
    - C. Cayenne

5. What does **victories** mean in this book?

Over the years, Porsche has won thousands of races. That includes many victories at Le Mans.

- **A.** jobs
- **B.** losses
- **C.** wins

6. What does **varieties** mean in this book?

Porsche sold several varieties of 718. The GTS had the most power. The Style Edition showed off striking colors and bodywork.

- **A.** different types
- **B.** exact copies
- **C.** fake names

Answer key on page 32.

GLOSSARY

accelerator
A pedal that controls the speed of a vehicle.

championship
A contest that decides a winner.

clinch
To make certain that something will be won.

concept car
A vehicle that shows new technologies or designs.

engineer
A person who uses math and science to solve problems.

Formula E
The highest level of open-wheel racing for electric cars.

mechanic
A person who works on and repairs machines.

production cars
Cars sold to the public and allowed to drive on public roads.

sedan
A car that seats at least four people comfortably.

TO LEARN MORE

BOOKS

Adamson, Thomas K. *Porsche Taycan*. Bellwether Media, 2023.

Colby, Jennifer. *Porsche*. Cherry Lake Publishing, 2023.

Hamilton, S. L. *Porsche*. Abdo Publishing, 2023.

ONLINE RESOURCES

Visit **www.apexeditions.com** to find links and resources related to this title.

ABOUT THE AUTHOR

Dalton Rains is a writer and editor from St. Paul, Minnesota. He would love to drive a Porsche someday.

#

356, 10
718, 20–21
911, 12, 16, 18, 20
917, 26
930, 13
963, 26

C

Cayenne, 14

F

Formula E, 4, 6–8

L

Le Mans, 9, 26

M

Macan, 14
Mission R, 25

P

Panamera, 15

T

Taycan, 22

V

Vision 357, 24

W

Wehrlein, Pascal, 4, 7–8

ANSWER KEY:
1. Answers will vary; 2. Answers will vary; 3. A; 4. A; 5. C; 6. A